Comfort
and Joy

Comfort and Joy

Christmas for the Soul

Mark-David Janus, CSP

Paulist Press
New York / Mahwah, NJ

Cover image by Artnizu / Shutterstock.com
Cover and book design by Lynn Else

Library of Congress Control Number: 2024938808

ISBN 978-0-8091-5751-8 (paperback)
ISBN 978-0-8091-8919-9 (ebook)

Published by Paulist Press
997 Macarthur Boulevard
Mahwah, NJ 07430
www.paulistpress.com

Printed and bound in the
United States of America

*In memory of my parents
Pearl and Casey
Who loved Christmas*

Contents

Preface
ix

PART 1
Twenty-Five Days to Christmas
1

PART 2
The Twelve Days of Christmas
63

Preface

CHRISTMAS IS TO BE CELEBRATED. We want Christmas to be charming for family and friends, and to be honest, I want a Happy Christmas as well. This depends on understanding why we celebrate the birth of Christ in the first place. Christmas is not a historical reenactment of the birth of the Christ Child. It is not even a day of remembrance as are so many of our national holidays. Christmas is the day we open our hearts to the One who has opened his heart to us. We make room in the noisy inn of our lives for the One who loves us—us—all of us.

These are not just pretty words—they make a difference in our lives—we are different because of Christmas. Being loved by God makes me who I am. As I open my heart to love, I become who I am supposed to be. Not only do I experience comfort and joy, I become comfort and joy for others.

This little book is divided into two parts. The first is the "Twenty-Five Days to Christmas." As a child I loved Advent calendars, searching for a little paper door behind which was a picture and a treat, heightening my anticipation for Christmas Day. Honoring this tradition are twenty-five reflections to heighten your Christmas readiness.

Comfort and Joy

The second part of the book is dedicated to "The Twelve Days of Christmas." The Christmas story is too rich to absorb in one day. We need at least twelve days to soak it all in, to revel in the multiple images and moments of the Christmas story.

Within these pages, may you find comfort and joy for your soul.

PART 1

Twenty-Five Days to Christmas

December 1

COMFORT

HANDEL'S *MESSIAH* BEGINS the Christmas season for me. I to listen to it, hopefully live, at least once before Christmas Day. I am entranced by the opening words, *"Comfort, Comfort my people!"* (Isa 40:1).

Give comfort this Christmas, sayeth the Lord.
My people are tired, battered, bruised, sore, wounded, hopeless, stressed.
They just manage to exist morning-to-night-to-morning-to-night—
the ceaseless cycle of their struggle repeats; life hard, unjust.

They have no sense of importance, no sense they make a difference,
affect change, create beauty. Their knowledge is discarded as straw,
their ethics, ridden over roughshod by brash, brawling liars.

Comfort and Joy

Narcissism is admired, violence a constant threat. My people's release—escape—is chemical oblivion, or perhaps, angry surrender to the wicked and selfish winning.

Comfort these people, my people, any way, every way, you can, with words that solace and soothe, encourage and praise. Weave afresh discarded dreams. Provide hot teas, saunas, flavorful foods, pillows for their heads, music for their souls, warm walls and a solid roof to keep them safe and dry.

My people need comfort; providing it is not easy. Pulling down mountains and filling in valleys is not milk and cookies. It means paying attention to the rough and tumble of somebody's day, someone's life.

Comfort means reading between the lines when told "I am fine." Above all, comfort means sacrificing my ease for another. Not that you don't deserve comfort; God wishes comfort for all, especially for purveyors of comfort.

There is in fact a special grace felt by the soul that reaches out to others
with comfort that is home: home—where they are known, loved, safe.
Home where they are challenged to live their belief out loud.[1]
Giving comfort for Christmas is crazy hard.
If you answer the call to comfort God's people, you are in for it.

---

1. I am indebted to Fr. Timothy Radcliffe, OP, for this description of home.

December 1

Those most in need of comfort are often those who resist its gift.

They have lost touch with themselves, flinching away from touch that comforts, choosing lonely substitutes that never suffice.

Who hasn't been so lost that we no longer know where we are headed or for what purpose? You might well think that entire countries, if not the whole world, have lost their way. Injustice, murder, greed, destruction—you think God wants that?

God is for the victim, not the murderer. God wants lies and deceit brought to light, not exchanged for truth. God wants the rights of ordinary people to count just as much as the rights of the strong. God does not want a future colored by evil, purchased and maintained by bloodshed. God sees all as equal—how did we create a world with some worth more than others?[2]

Providing comfort in these circumstances is more than sending thoughts and prayers. The comfort of justice, righteousness, honor—this comfort is hands-on, and years in the making. Giving this comfort is a lifetime well spent.

We are surrounded by different people, with various needs and circumstances, whose comfort takes different forms at different points in their lives. We do not have unlimited resources. What we do have, what we share with Jesus, is that we hear the same God calling, calling us to comfort God's people.

---

2. Walter Kasper, *Accepting the Mystery: Spiritual Reflections for Advent and Christmas* (Mahwah, NJ: Paulist Press, 2016), 5.

Comfort and Joy

What we share with Jesus is a Spirit, his Spirit, the Holy Spirit, the Comforter thumping inside our hearts. Instinctively, we are comfort givers, and mighty ones at that. We can give comfort. Each gift of comfort pulls down a mountain, fills in a valley, makes someone's path smoother and straighter—easier to find their way to the Christ born in Bethlehem.

December 2

WHY CHRISTMAS?

EVERYONE KNOWS CHRISTMAS is coming. If people know why Christmas is coming, well, that is another question. Christmas is memory:

We are the clay, You are our potter,
we are all the work of your hands. (Isa 64:8)

The hands that molded Jesus are the hands that molded us. We are made of the same clay, and God's fingerprints are all over our clay. Each with our own form, function, and color, sharing the same clay, the same stuff. We are none of us dispensable. We are all of us valuable.

We forget that—about ourselves and others. Perhaps because the King Herods of the world use us for their own purposes, discard us when finished, or smash us when we are chipped or cracked.

Advent is for remembering what God celebrates every Christmas:

Comfort and Joy

That we are, as is Jesus the Christ, precious. We are all precious.

Which is why we give gifts, send cards, and sing carols: to remind people that they are a gift, God's gift to us.

We give those gifts to those we love; we give gifts, clothes, toys, food

to people we will never meet, to people who may have forgotten that they are more than unemployed, poor, destitute, institutionalized, alone.

They are God's gift to us. God's fingerprints are all over them as they are all over the Christ. Since God's fingerprints are imprinted on our souls, we recognize the imprint of God's beauty in those that surround us as well as in the poorest, most ragged immigrant children who have no place to lay their heads.

More than a fair few of us receive no Christmas cards, no gifts, attend no parties. Yet, if we look at ourselves, we see God's imprint on our body and soul, formed of the same clay as the Christ.

That is Christmas.

December 3

JOHN THE BAPTIST

MEN ARE INFAMOUS for not asking for directions. Actually, no one loves direction from another. We each go our own way. Independent, self-reliant, self-directed, autonomous—that's how we think of ourselves. It is how the world wants us to be, how we must be—if we are to be successful, to survive in a competitive world.

The best of us—most renowned, ambitious, secure—from time to time are lost. Even while at home, we find ourselves in a wilderness we never wanted to visit, not at all sure how we got there, unable to find our way out.

Many voices cry in the wilderness; lonely, angry, wailing voices are swallowed up in a vast wilderness, going unanswered. Your wilderness looks different from mine. They are each unique. What they have in common is that none of us want to be there, and we do not know our way home.

In this wilderness is the biblical John the Baptist, coming in darkness, witnessing to light none of us can see. His voice cries out in the wilderness that there is a way out of the darkness we have driven ourselves into. There is a way home. But we cannot find it by ourselves. We have to stop and ask another for directions.

"Are you, do you, have the answer?" our Pharisee ancestors ask the Baptist.

"Do you know the way out, the way home? Are you the one we should be asking for directions?"

"No, I am not," the Baptist replies. The answers come from One who is to come.

Good News is found entirely in these words: No, I am not.

I am not the one with the answers.

I am not strong enough.

I am not wise enough.

I am not loving enough.

Maybe not even honest enough.

What the wilderness teaches is that I am not enough.

The simple admission that I am not enough

is the necessary step to see the light that leads me home.

John the Baptist has an uncomfortable but ultimately freeing message:

An essential part of my spiritual journey is acknowledging my need for others.

To the degree that I have convinced myself that to be a strong, admired, successful person I must rely on my own light and my own light alone.

To that degree will I ever remain in darkness.

Hurtling toward Christmas is the realization—I need a savior,

someone to point the way home, someone to walk with me on my journey.

Advent is an admission I spend my life avoiding: No, I am not, I am not enough.

Furthermore, I don't have to be, and am not supposed to be—alone.

I need something from the Christ I cannot get by myself.

In this season of shopping and celebrations, you may pass by churches glowing with light. Stop. Take a moment. Go in, just for a peek. Sit for a moment. There is Someone inside who knows who you are, where you are, and how to get you home where you belong.

December 4

WAITING

I am confident of this, that the one who began a good work among you will bring it to completion.

Paul to the Philippians (1:6)

God is at work in you, in me, in all of us.

That's a mystical thought: God, at work, in me.

I always think I am the one in charge,

the one in control, the one who makes all the decisions.

While it is true that the choices are always mine,

God never interferes with free will,

much of the inspiration belongs to God's love whispering in my heart.

How patient God is, waiting, waiting, waiting for me to have the courage to cooperate with the love within me.

Advent is often described as a time when we wait for God.

But perhaps Advent is a time when God is waiting for you.

Waiting for you to trust the love spoken into your heart.

Waiting for you to trust that you are strong enough to bring love and not selfishness into the world.

God is waiting for you to be confident enough in your heart that you share the best of yourself with those who are sharing only their worst. God is waiting for you to allow love to be reborn in your life.

This Advent season God is waiting for you, and will keep waiting,

waiting for you to complete the love begun when you were fashioned in the womb.

Like Paul, I am confident of this, and so should you be, confident, of God at work in you.

December 5

CHRISTMAS LISTS

WHAT DO YOU want for Christmas?

As children, all we had to do for Christmas was show up. We were the honored guests, the grateful recipients of the largess and preparations of others. Other people knocked themselves out for months, saving, spending, planning, decorating, buying, wrapping, menu designing, and cooking—basically for us.

We're the adults now, the hosts, creators, producers of Christmas for others, and for ourselves. What do you want for Christmas? I ask 'cause if you don't think about it, you're not going to get it. Your phones, laptops, tablets, and mailboxes are flooded with ideas about what you desperately need, cannot live without—guaranteed ecstasy. Hey, I like presents, they're fun. If you want to give me some—knock yourself out. This is beyond that.

What do you really, really want this Christmas? What is it you need to celebrate? Just who is it you want to gift with your love? What do you need that you cannot buy at a store or find for yourself? What do you need but do not have enough of—forgiveness, peace of mind, self-esteem, attention, recognition, comfort, touch? What above all do you wish you could do—laugh, dance, cry, hold another and be held in return, have beautiful things whispered in your ear, be made to feel lovely and loved? What difference do you want to make in the suffering that surrounds you? How do you encounter the mystery that is God?

What keeps you from having any or all of this? Much is out of our control. Forces larger than I, ill fortune, lack of opportunity or means all conspire against hopes. While all of that is true—at least for me—there is, I think, I hope, some little bit I can do. It may well be inconsequential when placed alongside my aspirations, but if I stop to think hard enough, stop long enough—to yearn, to pray—something within presents itself. Sadly, I am often the obstacle to overcome. Fear of being disappointed yet again stops me from another try. Brooding over injury, envy at others more gifted that easily grows into jealousy results in the growth of my inner Scrooge. There is an embarrassing proclivity to think that if I cannot have what I really want, I want nothing. If I cannot win the championship, why play? Better to slink home alone. Strange, isn't it, how alluring the temptation to nothing is?

Christmas asks you to squander time on your heart's desire. You are the only one who can rummage through your desires and select something authentic that deserves life. I will go so far as to say, this is God's Holy Spirit calling to you. It is annoyingly difficult to sort and choose what is possible within just a few weeks. Difficulty is no excuse. Nothing is impossible for God, so says Archangel Gabriel (Luke 1:37).

This searching and selection is how swords are beaten into plowshares and spears melted into pruning hooks (Isa 2:4). This is how humankind cleaves together to feed, house, and clothe one another with respect. This is how we learn, as St. Paul says, to owe one another only love, how we come to see strangers as fellow pilgrims on the path to God.

What do you want for Christmas?

December 6

ST. NIKOLAUS

THE FEAST OF St. Nikolaus is celebrated with parades, treats, sweets, and toys throughout much of northern and eastern Europe. Legends about this fourth-century Turkish bishop have traveled worldwide. A poor man with three daughters could afford no dowry for their weddings. Unmarried, they would be doomed to a life of ill repute. During the night, Nikolaus saves them from this fate by tossing through the window, or down the chimney, three bags of gold. On another occasion, hearing a wicked butcher had kidnapped and chopped up three boys and placed them in a tub of pickles, St. Nikolaus magically appears, smites the butcher, and miraculously restores the youths to life. In case you ever wondered why gold balls and pickles became ornaments to hang on the Christmas tree, wonder no longer. I am all for remembering Nikolaus as more than the forerunner of Santa Claus and recapturing his role as a saint and intercessor for children. Worthy of his place among the communion of saints, we need his prayers.

PRAYER TO ST. NIKOLAUS

St. Nikolaus, patron saint of children, thank you for the smiles, the joy, the delight your gifts bring. Your generosity directs our eyes to the child in the manger.

You are a protector of children, and many need your protection. Children who are poor, unloved, casualties and collateral damage in war, orphans, victims of abuse and trafficking, trapped in child labor without health care, education, nutrition—all defenseless.

Bless privileged children struggling with expectations creating anxiety, depression, and hopelessness.

Send your blessing on children who are ill, especially those near death.
Bless the children who have grown up tired, listless, lonely.

St. Nikolaus, your gifts, blessings, and example are enjoyed and needed more than ever. Give adults courage to follow in your footsteps, to multiply your blessings, so that all children find their way to the Child born in Bethlehem. Amen.

December 7

WE WISH YOU A MERRY CHRISTMAS

ANONYMOUSLY WE SCUTTLE by, without eye contact or acknowledgment, and so we make our way on the sidewalk, mall, and highway, hoping others will not get in our way. Oh, there are some who announce their presence loudly, conversing with people neither we nor they can see. This, the gift of a mobile phone. Often annoying and occasionally embarrassing, we are privy to an argument or an intimate conversation we wish they'd kept to themselves. They are not paying us attention, and we would rather not be forced to pay attention to them.

December threatens our unacknowledged passage through time when a stranger accosts us with the season's first: "Merry Christmas." Whence does this greeting come?

> The angel said to them, "Do not be afraid, for see—I am bringing you good news of great joy for all the people: to you is born this day in the city of David a Savior, who is the Messiah, the Lord. This will be a sign for you: you will find a child wrapped in bands of cloth and lying in a manger." (Luke 2:10–12)

The nativity has always needed angels to advertise God's love.

Theirs is the first "Merry Christmas." They had to explain what happened and why one more birth was a big deal, in fact, an occasion for joy, for glory.

December makes us angels, greetings of "Merry Christmas" our herald of Christmas love. People we do not know and may never see again merit our smile, blessing, and hope. The recipients of your greeting may not hear all that in "Merry Christmas." It is doubtful the shepherds understood everything the angels told them. They told them anyway.

Straighten your wings, embrace your angelic task, and let your "Merry Christmas" resound for friends and strangers to hear. Surprise them, as the shepherds were surprised, acknowledge them as someone worthy of a greeting. That is a gift people don't receive every day. Maybe someone just might go to the manger to see what you are talking about, and there find a child, wrapped in swaddling clothes, Christ the Lord.

Oh, I forgot to say, Merry Christmas!

December 8

IMMACULATE CONCEPTION

MARY ALWAYS POINTS to Jesus; like most mothers, it is never about her. Even the Feast of the Immaculate Conception is not about her, not really. The feast proclaims Mary is without original sin, which means Mary is the first to receive the privilege of being set free from that sticky spiderweb of sin and cynicism that so easily justifies our choosing dark paths. The rest of us receive that privilege from baptism in the faith of Jesus Christ, which replaces original sin with original love. Adam is not the moral head of the universe, Christ is. The inexorable doom of selfishness, called original sin, is not human destiny. It is possible to live a life of faith, hope, and love even as evil has its way over so many and so much.

Mary had hardships aplenty, more than enough to scar her soul, yet, when choices were possible, she chose love over fear, generosity over self-interest. Doing so cost her everything but love.

Where she has gone, we hope to follow.

We, too, can pick and weave a different path for ourselves and humanity.

It is not inevitable that we destroy the planet, and one by one, everyone on it.

We can give nurture and love life amidst and against darkness.

While our life has been touched, molded, and limited by the sins, selfishness, and failures of our fellow human beings, as well as our own, it is not who we are. The love of Christ sets us free to choose who and how we want to be.

Today we honor the heroine of original love by asking her to pray for our wavering footsteps as we travel on the path of her Son.

> *Hail Mary, full of Grace, the Lord is with thee.*
> *Blessed art thou amongst women,*
> *and Blest is the fruit of thy womb, Jesus.*
> *Holy Mary, mother of God, pray for us sinners,*
> *now and at the hour of our death, Amen.*

December 9

CHRISTMAS TREES 1

THE COLDEST DAY of December, preferably snowing if not sleeting, that is when my family went looking for our Christmas tree. Sloshing through the woods.

One tree looks much like any other when sheathed in snow. My parents scrutinized each for missing branches, a proper top, the right size—neither too tall nor too short, neither too round nor too slim. The axe clanging against frozen bark, the tree swooping to earth. We dragged our icicle to its perch atop the car, homeward bound. Enthroned in the corner or in front of the bay window, the thawing revealed that the tree was in fact crooked, possessed of gaping spaces between branches, its top stunted or spindly. No matter how deformed, each tree perfumed the house, and my dad loved it.

Our tree's deformities were soon sparkling with lights and tinsel, glittering with colored glass, protected by a moat of happily wrapped presents. If you grew up in the gray Northeast as I did, this green houseguest exuded hope, connecting us to a world too cold for outdoor play. The tree, a green angelic host, proclaiming our Savior's birth, reminding us how lucky we were to share life in a green world.

CHRISTMAS TREES 2

Green trees come to live in our house.
They know December is grim—
Dark, cloudy, wet.
Scraping ice off windshields,
Waiting, in the dark, for the bus
On the way in, on the way out.
Hassled in between, we struggle home to
Living rooms filled with green.
Sparkling light,
Ornaments a-glitter,
A sniff of spruce, fir, pine,
Soothing our battered soul
With wafts of hope.

December 10

NAUGHTY OR NICE

We think it is a choice, either/or.
Toys for the nice, coal for the naughty.
"So be good for goodness sake....Santa Claus is comin' to town."

I don't think it works that way.
To begin with, lots of the naughty have all the toys,
while lots of the good are lucky to have a lump of coal.
So that can't be how it works.

Christmas naughty and nice work like this:
Naughty and nice swirl inside as if we are candy canes.
We are both at the same time.

There is a way to increase your nice at the expense of
your naughty.
Picture in your mind's eye the part of yourself you most
despise.

The part you hide from your friends and don't discuss
with your spouse,

that secret sin that you do not confess to anyone;

memories of repugnant actions, personal and public shame,

your harshest rudest assessment of your personality,
character, self-worth.

Think of those parts too painful to think about,

those that lie beyond your forgiveness and acceptance,

beyond the acceptance and forgiveness of even those we
love.

Think on lack of courage and kindness, fear of love,

abundance of greed and arrogance.

Think of your practice of the seven deadliest of your sins.

Think of yourself at your very worst.

When you are as close to that as your soul will let you,

try accepting that you are welcomed,

embraced and enfolded in love made flesh called Christ.

This is what you celebrate at Christmas.

God's embrace of the naughty/nice of the human
condition is Christmas.

When you can accept that gift,

you will find it is easier to be good for Goodness sake.

Some religious traditions practice Advent[3] reconciliation.

You might give it a whirl, not to rehearse your inner
naughty,

but to be reminded, Christmas is God's gift to you.

_____

3. The Sacrament of Reconciliation is commonly known as Confession.

December 11

EBENEZER SCROOGE

*C*HRISTMAS WITHOUT Charles Dickens's *A Christmas Carol* is unthinkable, to me anyway. The team of Scrooge, Marley, Tiny Tim, and the Cratchits burst onto the Christmas stage in 1843 and has never been out of print. At its heart, it is a conversion story wherein Ebenezer Scrooge, *"a squeezing, wrenching, grasping, scraping, clutching, covetous old sinner...hard and sharp as flint from which no steel had ever struck out generous fire; secret, and self-contained, solitary as an oyster,"*[4] is converted through the ministrations of three ghosts. These are not just random ghosts; they are ghosts of Christmas past, present, and to come, who reveal the misery he has caused, the happiness he lost, and the joy others experience in celebrating the feast he casts aside with a "Bah! Humbug!"

The Ghost of Christmas Past is an especially subtle spirit, alternating dreadful and festive moments of Scrooge's past. Isn't it interesting when, hard-pressed by life, we are prone to forget our better moments? This psychologically astute ghost hurtles Scrooge back in time, when he was apprenticed to a jolly boss named Fezziwig, to the annual

---

4. Charles Dickens, *A Christmas Carol* (London: Chapman and Hall, 1843).

Christmas party. Scrooge watches the entire celebration before the Ghost intervenes:

> *"A small matter," said the Ghost, "to make these silly folks so full of gratitude."*
>
> *"Small!" echoed Scrooge.*
>
> *The Spirit signed to him to listen to the two apprentices, who were pouring out their hearts in praise of Fezziwig: and when he had done so, said,*
>
> *"Why! Is it not? He has spent but a few pounds of your mortal money: three or four perhaps. Is that so much that he deserves this praise?"*
>
> *"It isn't that," said Scrooge, heated by the remark, and speaking unconsciously like his former, not his latter, self. "It isn't that, Spirit. He has the power to render us happy or unhappy; to make our service light or burdensome; a pleasure or a toil. Say that his power lies in words and looks; in things so slight and insignificant that it is impossible to add and count 'em up: what then? The happiness he gives, is quite as great as if it cost a fortune."*

This tweaks my conscience. Do I make people happy or unhappy, their life a pleasure or toil, by the power of my words and looks, insignificant gestures that cost me nothing at all?

Christmas is more than the people with whom we share gifts and Christmas dinner. The Spirit of Christmas involves the relative strangers with whom I work, those absolute strangers whose paths I cross as I go about daily living. Happiness, gratitude, slight gifts perhaps—but as Scrooge reminds us, they are quite as great as if they cost a fortune.

December 12

OUR LADY OF GUADALUPE

"GO AWAY...WE don't want you here!" screamed a woman's voice from her car. She took time to roll down the window and bellow at a Latina immigrant woman and her children walking down the street near the shelter where they were housed. The incident captured on film by a local TV news team is not an isolated occurrence. That the derided mother brought her children here to escape falling into the hands of drug cartels made no difference to anyone.

Mary appeared as an Indian peasant, as Our Lady of Guadalupe. Mary seems to appear always to the downtrodden who are wanted nowhere. Patroness of the Americas, her feast is celebrated by tens of millions to whom she still speaks:

Am I not here, I, who am your Mother?

Are you not under my shadow and protection?

Am I not the source of your joy?

Are you not folded in my mantle?

Let nothing else worry or disturb you.

These words are a far cry from those screeched at the Latina mother. No wonder so many pray to her. Those of us favored with more material wealth might do well to pray to Our Lady of Guadalupe to increase the size of our hearts that we recognize in children of every color the Christ Child whose birth we celebrate this Christmas.

December 13

FEAST OF ST. LUCY

THE FEAST OF St. Lucy, in Sweden and, really, all of Scandinavia, is the start of the Christmas season. Lucia (whose name means *light*) would bring needed food and supplies to Christians hiding in the catacombs, which she navigated with a candle fixed to her head so both arms would be freed to carry goods.

According to Swedish legend, after her martyrdom in Rome, during which her eyes were removed, she appeared in Sweden as a maiden wearing white, with a red sash (symbol of martyrdom), crowned with light, distributing food and clothing to people. On the darkest day of the Swedish calendar, she does so again, accompanied by maidens, star boys, and gingerbread boys. Isn't it ironic that, in the land of the Vikings, it is a woman who is the first bringer of the Christmas message?

Today all Sweden is aglow in candlelight and special sweets. Light in the midst of darkness is an essential Christmas theme. Santa Lucia's light is found in caring for those in need, which, when you come to think of it, is a perfect celebration of Christmas.

St. Lucy the martyr asks me an uncomfortable question: is my generosity a light? Just how much discomfort will I endure to provide for the needs of others? The Christmas message is not just fa-la-la-la-la. Christmas is a light that makes it possible for me to see people who are usually unseen, living in the shadows of my attention.

December 14

CANDLE IN THE DARK

Perhaps this year you have no energy for Christmas celebrations.

Loss does that.

Loneliness does that.

Illness does that.

Rejection does that.

Unemployment, homelessness, grief drain the fa-la-la-la.

War and its depravities scorn a Merry Christmas.

We know people this is happening to.

Maybe we are the people this is happening to,

right now, this year, today.

Hope and all its carols ring hollow in our ears.

If anything, accentuating our pain.

The heart of Christmas is light in darkness.

Christmas is lighting one single candle against a starless night.

December 14

It may not make us feel better,
but it will remind us darkness is not all there is.
Somewhere inside us we cannot reach
hopes for touch, for love, for laughter,
for the chance to befriend ourselves once again.

It is not tinsel, or glitter. It is not cozy.
It is not accompanied by rich smells from the kitchen.
But lighting one candle keeps us from oblivion,
keeps us alive for better times.

Light in darkness is who the Christ Child is.
Light for our darkness.

December 15

CHRISTMAS CARDS

*The voice of my beloved! Look, he comes, leaping
upon the mountains,*

bounding over the hills.

My beloved is like a gazelle or a young stag.

*Look, there he stands behind our wall gazing
in at the windows,*

*looking through the lattice. My beloved speaks
and says to me,*

"Arise my love, my fair one, and come away!"

Song of Solomon 2:8–14

A BIT RACY FOR the Christmas card you might say; nonetheless, another biblical image for the coming of the Messiah. If the little Lord Jesus asleep in the hay does not do it for you, try this one, intimate, passionate, Christ the gazelle who adores you!

"Come, let us adore," we sing, but have you ever thought we got it the wrong way round? Christ is born calling you: *"My beautiful, my lovely one, my dove, my beloved. Arise and come!"* Try thinking about that, and you will know something about Christmas you did not know before.

December 16

CHRISTMAS LIGHTS

MY GREAT-GRANDPARENTS lit candles in the window on Christmas Eve to signal the wandering Christ Child that theirs was a house of welcome, searching for blessing. My grandfather, fulfilling his dream with the purchase of his own home in Buffalo, was not content with one candle. From roof to lawn, electric lights were gratefully strewn throughout the entire Christmas season. Houses gleaming with Christmas lights decorate my memory. Packed into my dad's unheated car, my family drove through neighborhoods, oohing and ahhing at their decorated splendor.

Some homes were simply adorned in white lights, while others fizzing in multicolor like a new box of crayons. Stately mansion windows ornamented themselves with wreaths and ribbons. Less presupposing houses unabashedly displayed glowing Santa, reindeer, snowmen. Peaceful houses dressed all in blue. Religious dwellings provided ready room on their lawns for Mary, Joseph, and the Babe in the manger. Inexpensive entertainment announcing joy as surely as any angelic host. All of this, provided by people inside the house who seldom catch sight of the happiness they create for the pleasure of strangers.

The last Christmas of my mother's life, multiple strokes stole her mobility and speech. One December night I bundled her into a car, and we went for a drive to look at Christmas lights. Some simply white, others multicolored, or only blue. Windows wrapped in red bows, lawns peopled by shining snowmen, Santa, elves, even the Christ Child, Mary, Joseph, attended by glowing sheep, shepherds, and Magi.

Since my mother could not speak, I kept up a running commentary about each display. My mother, not a physically affectionate woman, surprised me as she reached across to hold my hand as we drove. Her last and maybe best Christmas present for me.

I am ever grateful to those who decorate their homes. They put me in mind of so many unknown people whose efforts make Christmas sparkle: carol singers, musicians, store clerks, tree farmers, those who put on local Christmas theater, teachers who organize children's Christmas pageants.

Who bakes all those cookies and cakes? Where do these poinsettias come from? Gatherers of toys for children bereft of them, generous carvers of turkeys for those without, are angels in disguise.

It won't take you long to add to your own list of anonymous Christmas benefactors. The cynical say they contribute to Christmas commercialism. I prefer to thank them.

I think we are all shepherds working the night shift, unaware something spectacular is happening. In their own little way, these varied Christmas angels remind us of God's glories born around us.

December 17

ANNUNCIATION

"Be it done unto me according to thy word."...Then the
angel departed.

Luke 1:38 (author's translation)

Well, what choice did she have?

We are always having things done unto us.

It doesn't seem as if God spends much time asking
whether we want to be done unto or not.

Nobody gets to be asked about being in the path
of a hurricane, earthquake, fire, or flood.

Nobody asks to be a victim in a war, or a drive-by
shooting.

Nobody's life goal is to be exploited,

or have a career as the victim of crime or prejudice.

So where does Mary get off, having her own personal
archangel,

asked if she wants a say in her destiny?

I don't have much predictive or explanatory information
about tragedies befalling us except to say,

God only wills good for us.
God does not send disasters into our life as a pop quiz,
to see if we are paying attention.

What I do know is this,
when faced with the opportunity to do good,
when the opportunity to create justice is in our reach,
when the opportunity for love appears,
God asks our permission.
God can only invite us to the dance; we cannot be made
to go.
We cannot be made to love God.
We cannot be made to love ourselves.
We cannot be made to love anyone else.
The Almighty, All-Powerful, Omnipotent God
can only ask if we want to come out and play.

In W. H. Auden's *For the Time Being: A Christmas Oratorio*, the Angel Gabriel lyrically asks Mary:

"What I am willed to ask, your own will has to answer;
Child it lies within your power of choosing
To conceive the Child who chooses you."[5]

---

5. W. H. Auden, *For the Time Being: A Christmas Oratorio* (New York: Random House, 1944).

Comfort and Joy

It is Mary's choice; she can make it so, or not. She has no special qualification, no training, no experience to call upon in her decision. Too young to drive a car, Almighty God entrusts her with salvation. Apparently, you do not have to be very old to be asked to give birth to love.

Neither age nor inexperience disqualify us from God's invitation to add our love to

creation's history. Nor are we backed into a corner and made to submit.

Love must always be chosen, even and perhaps especially, at Christmas.

Fourteenth-century spiritual writer Meister Eckhart challenges,

"If Christ is not born again within your own soul,
What possible difference can his historical birth mean to you." [6]

To which I say, Ouch! Must you be so blunt?

Somewhere in the hectic season Advent/Christmastide has become,

an inconvenient angel will whisper a question,

"Will you allow God to be done unto your heart,

be born of your flesh,

appear to others in your life?"

The answer is yours.

---

6. Meister Eckhart, *Dum Medium Silentium* 18:14, authors translation.

December 18

JOSEPH

An angel of the Lord appeared to him in a dream and said,

"Joseph, son of David, do not be afraid to take Mary as your wife,

for the child conceived in her is from the Holy Spirit."

Matthew 1:20

JOSEPH:[7] I LOVED Mary. She was so special! I wanted to marry her, to be with her forever. I dreamt of running my fingers through her hair, of waking up each morning to her eyes. I said to myself, "Joseph, you are a lucky man! God has blessed you. God has given Mary to love you." If you had only known her, you would know what I mean. One day she came to visit me, quite risqué in those times.

"Mary, what are you doing here? It's good to see you!"

---

7. This is a fictional psychological reconstruction entirely of my own making. I am attempting to grapple with Joseph's decision. The scriptures have no interest in his psychology, only his behavior.

Comfort and Joy

"Talk—I want nothing else but to talk to you."

It was then that she told me.

"Pregnant? Pregnant! You don't know how?

Mary, everyone knows how. It isn't how; it's who!

God?"

She told me God. Would you believe that?

She was so small then, trembling, beautiful through her tears.

I couldn't stand it. I couldn't stand that someone else kissed her.

Someone else touched her. Someone else woke up alongside her.

I couldn't stand that she would bear someone else's child.

What I really couldn't stand is that I would never kiss her.

Never touch her; she'd never be mine; she'd never have my child.

I ran out of my house.

People would know soon. We are a small town, people know everything. The more intimate the thing, the more they want to know it. They would hurt her.

Yank her in her bedclothes, drag her through town, spitting, yelling, calling her names, driving her beyond the gates, stone her with rocks till they crush her skull and she has no more blood to soak the ground.

NO, NO, NO! I'll divorce her, take her to where no one knows us and divorce her there, quietly. Of course, once I do that, no one will marry her, she'll never have a home of her own. She'll be someone's servant—to do with as they fancy.

You see, I had to choose, how she would live, how she'd die. I had no good choices, no choices of my own. No matter what I did, she'd be hurt. I'd be hurt.

I did not sleep at first, then restlessly, finally, with dreams. Dreams talk to you, tell you about yourself. They are messages: some from demons, some from angels. One night, in a dream, an angel came to me.

"Joseph, do you love Mary?"

"Yes."

"Do you love her?"

"Yes."

"Do you love Mary?"

"Yes, yes, yes!"

"Does she love you?"

"Yes."

"Is love from God?"

"Yes."

"Joseph, this child is from God. Do not be afraid. Trust her. Love her. Take this child into your home."

What could I do? I loved Mary.

A child is a frail creature. It needs nurturance, protection, affection. It needs someone to believe in it. Someone who hopes enough in its future to invest in it, to sacrifice for it. A child needs someone to love it, someone who allows themselves to be loved by the child. The Christ child, no matter how old we are, is part of us, needing from us what he needed from Joseph:

Someone willing to give their love away for the sake of another. That is the only way God is born, then, and now.

December 19

CHRISTMAS TRAVEL

TRAVEL IS PART of Christmas, over the river and through the woods and all that to Grandmother's house, or someone's house....Far away or to the neighbor next door. Perhaps you travel to no one's house but rather a ski lodge, a beach, a cruise ship. Going somewhere to celebrate with somebody even if you don't know them.

If you are traveling this Christmas, you are in good company. The first Christmas was a journey—Mary and Joseph to Bethlehem. Followed by Magi whose Google Map was a star.

Travels continue, Santa Claus and his reindeer, St. Nicholas riding his horse,

Befana riding a broom or trudging roads. Once I spent all of Christmas Day on a train, and more than once, all the sainted day in airports going nowhere.

If you are traveling this Christmas, be patient, with yourself, with your traveling companions, with those you meet on the way. Be patient when you arrive; don't just be patient—be safe. Early or late—the point is to arrive without turning into the Grinch that stole Christmas. Those waiting for you will wait.

Traveling is part of Christmas, going from where we are to someplace else; from selfishness to generosity, self-absorption to the joy of another.

If traveling days are behind you and you remain behind in a nursing home, hospital bed, or apartment with none to visit and none to visit you, you and I can travel in our dreams, memories of Christmases past in which we can live gratefully. We can travel on the wings of hope, carried by the winds of prayer to the Christ who travels still to be with us.

December 20

CHRISTMAS VISITORS

Mary set out and went with haste to a Judean town in the hill country,

where she entered the house of Zechariah and greeted Elizabeth.

Luke 1:39

RELATIVES VISIT DURING the holidays. This is the story of Elizabeth, an elderly woman, miraculously pregnant, six months pregnant in fact. Elderly, uncomfortable, and very pregnant, she is to be visited by her thirteen-to-fourteen-year-old cousin, who is also miraculously pregnant, so she insists. Mary is coming to visit for three months. This is just what every elderly pregnant woman wants: a three-month visit from a pregnant teenaged relative. Can't you just imagine the "yippie" Elizabeth shouts when she hears about this visit?

However, Elizabeth is not an ordinary woman, nor is Mary an ordinary visitor, and theirs are not ordinary pregnancies. These are women who believe that God is active in their lives; women who believe God is part of ordinary life, ordinary events, like birth, like death.

Christmas is a time for visitors and visiting. Sometimes we visit, sometimes we are visited. Some visitors we see only at Christmas, for which we are very grateful. We only invited them because we thought they wouldn't come.

Some visitors are a sight for sore eyes, the life of the party, uncles and aunts who like Uncle Drosselmeyer of *The Nutcracker*[8] make the most amazing things happen. Some are the children and grandchildren waited for with more anticipation than for Christmas itself. Some visitors are unexpected, surprisingly helpful; some end up as in-laws.

Sometimes we are the visitors. Visiting is a skill, knowing what to say and what not to say, taking care to talk neither too little nor certainly too much. Knowing where to sit, what place at table is yours and which is already claimed, is a skill. How to be comfortable but not intrude, observing with interest but never criticizing the bizarre local customs of the house. Sometimes we visitors are constantly thinking of just how soon we can politely make our escape.

Sometimes we are so much more loved, appreciated, and happy where we visit than we are at home that we cannot bear to head for the door. Overstaying our welcome seems a less grievous sin than returning to the dark place where we belong.

Sometimes visitors and visiting are only Christmas memories: events from the past that cannot be repeated in the present. We can no longer go, others no longer come, but we remember it all; sometimes fondly, sometimes with sadness.

"Who am I that the mother of my Lord should come to me?" rejoices Elizabeth.

We might well ask, who am I that my Lord comes to me

---

8. *The Nutcracker* is a ballet set to music by Tchaikovsky, and is a perennial holiday favorite, even for people who do not enjoy ballet.

Comfort and Joy

in another? Who am I to bring the Lord to others? Who are we? We are not ordinary people either.

We are people like Mary and Elizabeth in whose lives God is active.

Throughout this week and through all the twelve days of Christmas you will visit or be visited or remember visits long passed. In all the coming and the going this week as well as the longing and memories of visits long ago, I can only promise you this: Christ will be there. Christ will be there for us to bring, and for us to receive. Even in the absence of people to visit or people to visit us, Christ will visit us in our hearts. As old Elizabeth says: *"Blessed are you who believe that the word spoken to you by God will be fulfilled!"*

December 21

BLUE CHRISTMAS

YOU ARE TIRED of Christmas already. All you want is to sleep until it is all over.

The Christmas bling does not sparkle for you. Carols do not sing in your heart. Church makes you feel empty, not holy. While you would never dare tell anyone, the sight of all these happy people, excited for Christmas family and friends, makes you lonely and sad. You don't begrudge them happiness, but please, leave you out of it. For Christ's sake, you don't want to explain yourself to someone who tries to get you to feel differently.

You are who you are. Do they think you want to feel the way you do? That you wouldn't change it if you could? Do they think you haven't tried? History matters, your life story can't be wiped clean by jingle bells. Your Christmas memories are not like theirs. Disappointment, pain, violence, trauma—those haunt your Christmas. Who wants to bring all that up again?

If, once upon a time, Christmas was magic, it isn't now. If they knew who you lost, how the person who made

Comfort and Joy

Christmas special for you vanished, they wouldn't be poking you about Merry Christmas.

If they lived in your body, where mist shades all tinsel and lights, and Christmas punch is a cocktail of one pill after another, none of them working for long, they wouldn't be telling you to snap out of it. If they lived with your pain, they would know 'tis not the season to be jolly. You couldn't go to a Christmas concert or Midnight Mass any more than you could fly to the moon.

I don't know what makes you feel the way you do—there is no shortage of reasons, no shortage of pain. I am not going to try to talk you out of it.

If I could make you better, I would. But I can't. I do have a few ideas, take them if you want.

Don't blame yourself for not being in the Christmas mood. You do not need to feel worse about yourself than you already do. You are doing the best you can.

Gently excuse yourself from social situations where you will be miserable.

If people are upset you didn't show up for Christmas dinner, that is their problem, not your fault.

Don't go to a church mobbed with people if that makes you nervous. If you do go, and you can't get yourself to pray, no worries, let them pray for you. That's what a church is for, to pray for us, when we can't pray for ourselves.

It might help to slip into church when no one is there. Sit there a while, just you and God. You don't have to say or think or feel anything if you don't want to. Being there is enough.

Don't drink a lot of alcohol; it doesn't help—it really doesn't. Neither does meth, heroin, or cocaine if you use those. If you don't, now is not the time to start.

Don't be all alone if you can help it. If you have a friend, someone you can talk to, arrange to get together and watch a movie or something before or after Christmas.

If you have a therapist, make an appointment for right after Christmas, even if just on the phone or by Zoom.

On Christmas Day itself, Chinese restaurants are filled with nice Jewish people who won't bother you about Christmas. They are waiting for it to be over too.

If you have the energy, and that's a big if, food kitchens always need help serving the poor. You won't be alone, and it will do some good.

Finally, while this may not take away your pain, you are the reason Christ is born, to share your suffering. It will not always be this bad, but while it is, the Risen Christ shares it with you. You are not alone. You are not unloved. There is no place you can go where God will not find you and love you. Try to hang on to that as best you can, and if it slips away, read this page again.

December 22

SHEPHERDS

IF AS A CHILD you were ever drafted into the school or church Christmas pageant, odds are you were a shepherd. In such a small nonspeaking part, you could do little to damage the performance. It is a good metaphor; most of us travel through life in a nonspeaking role, not likely to damage life's performance. That's how we like it. However, each Christmas we shepherds are bothered by angels, intruding into our peaceful field, turning our attention to some strangers' Child. What a fuss!

I am bringing you good news of great joy for all the people:

To you is born this day in the city of David a Savior, who is the Messiah, the Lord.

This will be a sign for you: you will find a child

wrapped in bands of cloth and lying in a manger.
(Luke 2:10–13)

If you think about it, unless angels called attention to his birth, the Bethlehem shepherds would neither notice nor care that Jesus was born. Even when they arrived at the place, they wondered what all the fuss was about.

They saw no Savior, not as we think of one anyway; no one all-powerful, almighty someone to inspire them and awe their enemies. They saw only a child, wrapped in swaddling clothes, as all children are, laid in the straw as poor children are. They saw someone who looked just like they did when they were children. They saw someone who looked just like their children.

Yearly, angels draw our attention to the same place and to the Child who still looks no different from any other child. Like the shepherds before us we wonder what the fuss is about. God, we expect, comes in a bigger package, a more impressive present that would dazzle us, frighten our enemies, and make us the envy of all. But all we get is the infant, wrapped in swaddling clothes, lying in a manger.

From this manger, Christians take away a life-changing truth. We believe that God is in this Child, accessible to all, not desiring to be feared, just loved.

Human beings do not have to struggle to reach God; God's love has already reached us. All we have, all we ever will be, is embraced and shared by God who will now, as then, whether we know it or not, continue to share our life, celebrate our joys, receive our tears, share our anxieties, now and especially at the hour of our death.

Coming to human beings, through human beings, is the central point of Christian faith, and only eyes glistening with faith will see in that Child the presence of their Savior.

Those of us shepherds who, however dimly, hear the angelic message and focus our attention on the child who is God's gift to us, then ever after will look on every child, even homeless immigrant children, differently than before. We will see them as God's gift to us, the way God continues to come to us, through human beings.

That is what all the fuss is about.

December 23

MARY

"Hail Mary, Full of Grace, The Lord is with you."

With Christmas so close, we can taste it. Take a deep breath,
and for a few moments think of Mary—you know, Mary.
She's on all the Christmas cards and in the nativity sets.
Mary, not a superhuman wonder woman, but Mary,
as model for believing in and celebrating the birth of Jesus
as the Christ.

Sit back, close your eyes if you will, and in your mind's eye,
place yourself in her shoes, and as the angel says to her,
"Hail Mary; Blest are you!"
insert your name—John, Sue, Celeste, Camille, Caleb—
Blest are you! God is calling you by name, God has always been calling you.
God never stops calling you.

God never forgets you.

Once God has your attention, Gabriel will say to you, as to Mary,

"The Lord is with you. Do not be afraid. You have found favor with God."

Grace follows you your whole life, whether you feel it or not.

Whether you believe it, or not—God believes in you.

God should know; God made you; God knows the love you carry within.

God knows you better than you know yourself.

Soak that in.

If, as did Mary, you can accept those words as true,

if, as did Mary, you can allow God's love for you to define your life,

you are well on your way to living Christmas.

There is a catch, there is always a catch, even angels have fine print.

God's love is a living thing, a verb, not a noun.

It is not my personal property; it is a gift, a Christmas present,

to be given away to others, Light in their darkness,

Hope when all is hopeless.

On Christmas Day, and throughout the twelve days of Christmas

Do your best to accept God's love in your heart, and then,

Give it away as your Christmas present to all you meet.

December 24

CHRISTMAS EVE

UNDER THE CHRISTMAS tree, or on a fireplace mantle, or in some other place of honor, the nativity set appears on Christmas Eve. The invention of St. Francis, these figurines, majestic or humble, remind us of that first Christmas, when the newborn Child Jesus was laid in a manger. A few rough planks of wood are all that kept a newborn Jesus from the cold ground. It was the best his homeless, immigrant parents could do.

Extreme, perhaps, but not unusual. There are neighborhoods where newborn babies are laid to sleep in bureau drawers, keeping them off the floor. It is the best their parents can do. Stretching the metaphor, only a little, a few sheets of cardboard are all that come between homeless people, who were once someone's child, and the heating grates they sleep on. Only a few planks of wood come between Syrian children and the Mediterranean Sea. Like Mary and Joseph before them, it is the best these Middle Eastern parents can do fleeing war and persecution. Families escaping Mexican drug lords put their children to sleep on the bare ground. Which is where many Venezuelan children with no place to go to escape starvation also sleep.

The manger is not limited to literal interpretation. There are times we are all flat on our backs with nothing or next to nothing between us and the earth. Broken relationships, unemployment, disappointment, loneliness, injustice, a broken body wracked with illness that will not quit, depression, anxiety, Alzheimer's torturing the mind, the death of loved ones, the specter of our own death— any one of these and we are flat on our backs with precious little to protect us from cold earth.

We rest on planks of wood because of rejection, created by the color of our skin, the language we speak, the country we come from, how old we are, the gender we love, the God we pray to. In those moments when we have nothing, when we are nothing, Jesus is right alongside, sharing our scrap of wood.

Our God is a God of human beings. When the free will God has given humankind is used to exploit, to wound, to make a profit off the misfortune of another; when free will fails to pay attention, to take notice, to feel for and feel with the pain of another; when the mystery of life leads our bodies to decay from this life to enter the next; when one human being chooses to kill another, then the wooden slats of the manger are formed into a cross. God's mercy fixes himself to our cross, and we are not alone.

Nor is God's mercy limited to our length of days. The injustice suffered is remembered in heaven where there is no hunger or thirst; where the tears are wiped from our eyes and God's love surrounds us forevermore. The scraps of the manger's wood remind us God does not wait to be invited into our lives but comes on His own, sharing our most difficult moments.

We celebrate the manger because it tells us who God is: Emmanuel, God with us. We celebrate the manger because it foretells our future when we will be with God forever. We celebrate the manger because it tells us who we are: people so deserving of love that God became one of us.

In defiance of Caesar Augustus, who counted people only that they might be taxed, used, and sacrificed, God became a human being because each human being is God-worthy of love. God believes, even if we do not, that human beings are made in God's image and likeness.

So, we are none of us measured by the planks of wood that describe our suffering. We are all of us measured only by the love that prompted Jesus to crawl into each of our mangers and in so doing proclaim what we cannot make ourselves believe—that in God's merciful eyes, we are worth all the love God can give, worth Jesus's life, worth his death, worth joining in His resurrection.

In churches throughout the world, in fields where there are no churches, in places where churches are forbidden, in basements and caves, Christians at midnight, morning, and during the day gather around the manger that held the Christ Child, singing at the top of our voices of the Love of God who choose then and for all time to share our life that we might for all time share His life. Each carol sung, each candle lit, each prayer uttered, each gift exchanged, each meal shared is a witness of comfort and joy.

But they are more than that. Our Christmas celebration is an act of defiance against Caesar Augustus and his kind—against all who measure, use, and abuse human life for their gain and their purpose. In every place Christians gather tonight, we stand with the Christ who came to the manger to stand with us. We stand with all those who are dishonored, disregarded, deprived of the love and dignity that is theirs by God's gift. We stand against all who would take that gift from them. We stand with the angels announcing great tidings of joy to be shared by all:

Unto you a Savior has been born—He is Christ the Lord,
And you will find him lying in a manger,

And with Him and for you is the Glory of God. (Luke 2:11, 12, 14 [author's translation and abbreviation])

Merry Christmas.

P.S. Don't forget to put out the milk and cookies for Santa.

December 25

PEACE ON EARTH

I WAS IN ROME, attending a conference on interfaith dialogue. A Jewish representative spoke about faith and security. A Muslim representative spoke of oppression and displacement. Then a Palestinian Christian spoke, the Roman Catholic bishop of Nazareth. The tiny man, Archbishop Elias Chacour addressed the council, his powerful voice thundering:

"I thank God I was not born a Jew.

"I thank God I was not born a Muslim.

"I thank God I was not born a Christian.

"I thank God I was born a baby."

Before we were Christians, Muslims, or Jews, Hindus, Buddhists, atheists, or agnostics, we were all babies, all born alike, loved and fashioned in the image and likeness of the God born just as are we. Christmas reminds us of God's embrace of humanity. People of every race, every language, every way of life—rich, poor, black, white, yellow, brown, straight, gay, young, old, sinner, saint, married, single, famous, unknown, talented, struggling, healthy, diseased—belong to God. Since we all belong to God, like it or not, we belong to one another.

Even now, we find it hard to see past complexion to community. Labels make us enemies. Many a Christmas dinner is tense with family division. Religious strife is so prevalent that many conclude religion itself is the cause of violence, not the solution.

We celebrate Christmas, sometimes grandly, sometimes simply; even while impoverished we celebrate. Sometimes we are surrounded by loved ones. Sometimes, all by ourselves. Even so, the angelic good news of great joy is for all the people: we are part of one another. God is with *us*, all of *us*. Not just me by myself, gathered around the tree with my family and friends, but all of us. Not just the people I understand and agree with but the people whom I just can't get, whose experiences and views are foreign and perhaps frightening to me.

Each Christmas God gives us the same gift, a child lying in a manger. If we see the Christ Child as God with us, we see every child as God's love, crying out for us to live in Peace.

PART 2

The Twelve Days of Christmas

Introduction

I DO NOT UNDERSTAND people who throw their Christmas tree to the curb on December 26, as if Christmas is over, done and dusted. Christmas is the Christian dealbreaker. For Orthodox Christianity, Christmas is as important as Easter. I don't think it is possible to absorb the spiritual depths of the Christmas message in one day. Christmastide is the period between Christmas Day and the Feast of Epiphany, celebrated on January 6. It allows for a more complete reflection on the impact of the Christmas message.

Pardon the play on words, but these are days for meditating on what your true Love has given you, and what you do with it.

First Day of Christmas

December 25

CHRISTMAS NIGHT

CHRISTMAS NIGHT IS a deep collective sigh. The presents are opened, the leftovers are in the refrigerator, the dishes—well, they can wait till morning. Remains of the meal are put away, new toys are put to their use, and relatives are on their way home, leaving you to settle down with a relaxing beverage. The hard work of the Christmas celebration has, for today, come to an end.

Ever wonder what the original second night of Christmas was like?

Angelic hosts had long faded silently into the dark; curious shepherds returned to their work keeping watch over their flocks by night.

I like to think word got around, and some woman from the village came with fresh water, straw, and swaddling clothes to clean Mary and make her baby comfortable.

First Day of Christmas

In my mind's eye, I see Joseph standing guard at the cave entrance.

Wolves could hungrily smell a new birth on which to prey; he dare not leave them unprotected even to get food.

Perhaps a shepherd returned with goat cheese, milk,

maybe a piece of cold lamb, provisions to get the couple through the night.

But what then? What would happen then? The excitement was over.

The work of surviving had just begun.

These are the worries of ordinary parents, like yours and mine,

the ordinary worries you have for your loved ones. That the parents of the Christ and the Christ himself share the same risks and troubles, the same burdens, worries, and dangers as anyone else is the point of Christmas.

God is with us in our comings and goings,

our woes and worries, delights and hopes, loves and losses.

Christ is with us for the same reasons we want to be with anybody we love—

to find joy and comfort in their company, to stand by them in their sorrows, to heal their wounds, rejoice in their accomplishments.

God with us, as we wish to love and be loved, on any ordinary night, not unlike the night when God's glory shone over our uncertain future.

Comfort and Joy

Wanting for us the justice that gives us the space to love and to be,

the security and peace, so people of goodwill can play and rest.

When all the splash and bling are gone, what remains with us here in the dark

is the Christ, the Christ who will be with us on every step of life's journey.

With us in our times of trial, with us in our excitements and joys, with us even when our steps leave this life behind to journey to the other side of heaven.

Honestly, I don't know what it was like for Mary, Joseph, and the Christ Child,

that second night of Christmas. But I do know that that night was just like this one,

and now, no less than it was then, the truth is, the Lord of Love is with you.

Second Day of Christmas

December 26

MARY'S SONG OF THANKS (LUKE 1:46–55)

My spirit rejoices.

Luke 1:47

Memories of glittering packages,
an impenetrable moat of anticipation protecting our
Christmas tree,
is an easy memory.
Less precise are recollections of their contents.
If I dig deep enough, only once do I remember receiving
exactly what I wanted: a plastic castle, complete with
drawbridge, knights, and dragons. (I aspired to a career as
a knight at the Round Table).

Comfort and Joy

My memory is cluttered with smaller delights:
Tangerines, plastic Roman soldiers, dime-store treasures:
chess sets, checkers, popguns, hockey pucks, rubber balls,
golf balls, tiny switch knives,
all painstakingly wrapped and ribboned.

Presents were opened one at a time, round-robin, starting
with the youngest,
with each gift, the tall and the small, receiving oohs and
ahhs from an attentive circle.

These sidebars of stories and jokes wrapped my neurons
around the idea
that what I gave to others was more worthy of attention
than what I hoped to receive.

"He has filled the hungry with good things" (Luke 1:53).
We had three Christmas celebrations:
Christmas Eve with paternal grandparents,
Christmas Day—the maternal grandparents,
and the day after, at our house.
My tongue remembers Nanas with contrasting styles
of culinary delight, demanding copious amounts be
consumed
ever before a present was opened, a tradition my mother
continued
when she graduated into Nana-hood.

One Nana, a dish towel draped over her shoulder,
continually circled the table

with morsels fresh from her kitchen, never reluctant to snap the towel

across your shoulders if she gauged talking exceeded chewing.

"He has helped his servant Israel, in remembrance of his mercy" (Luke 1:54).

One by one, people essential to Christmas passed on to join harking angels, leaving us in grief to regroup, reimagine our celebration of Christmas

when they no longer circled the tree and table.

This we did, remembering each one missed was God's promise of mercy gracing our lives—indelible memories of their peculiar brand of love.

Their mercies feed me still, as do all the lives that have taken their place

around my Christmas tree, each life a glittering present

waiting to be opened, an occasion for Mary and me to sing:

"My soul magnifies the Lord" (Luke 1:46).

Third Day of Christmas

December 27

FRIENDS

Her parents had just finished putting her to bed:
drink of milk, bedtime story,
tucking in the covers, good-night kiss—all done.
They turned off the lights, softly closed the door,
and were walking down the hall
when they heard her cry out as if she were in trouble.
Hurrying in, they asked whatever could be the matter.
She said she was afraid.

It was dark, she was alone, afraid.
Nothing will hurt you, they reassured her.
"And you are never alone; you know God is always with
you."

Third Day of Christmas

"I know God is always with me," she replied,

"but tonight, I need God with skin on."[1]

So do we all;

we all need God with skin on.

Love in the abstract is a nice idea, but

we need a God we can touch, who touches us.

That is why we have the little Lord Jesus, asleep in the hay,

God with skin on, skin just like ours, hungering to touch and be touched.

This is who friends are, or should be: God with skin on.

During Christmas friends seek each other out,

A scattered but chosen family with whom we are safe.

Robert Frost described home as the place that,

When you have to go there, they have to take you in,

A place "you somehow haven't to deserve."[2]

If we are lucky, friends take us in when we need them most.

When we need to play, to celebrate, to dance, we look to friends.

When we have to rest, cry, complain, we look to friends.

When we need to just sit there, silent, saying nothing,

That is what friends do.

---

1. This story is embedded in the universal preaching Rolodex. I wish I could take credit for it, but I happily share it instead.

2. Robert Frost, "Death of a Hired Man," in *North of Boston* (London: David Nutt, 1914).

Comfort and Joy

Christmas is a time for visiting friends.
Friends are God's Christmas gift to us, God with skin on.
Through them, the Risen Lord touches us.
Through them we touch the divine.

"There is no greater love than to lay down your life
for your friends," Jesus, says.

Jesus is the original God with skin on, the touch of God
for us,
"Word of the Father now in flesh appearing," as the carol
sings.
He brings the touch of God in faith, hope, and love,
in endless mercy, and sacrificial love.
We model our friendship on his for us.

During Christmas, we celebrate God with skin on—
born in Bethlehem, born throughout time,
born in friends who make life worth living.

Fourth Day of Christmas

December 28

SLAUGHTER OF THE HOLY INNOCENTS

Herod is about to search for the child, to destroy him....he sent and killed all the children in and around Bethlehem who were two years old or under.

Matthew 2:13, 16

I BET YOU HAVEN'T read that verse on any Christmas card. We don't sing any Christmas carols about this part of Christmas. The Christmas story is not as sentimental, not as cozy, as we think it is. In St. Matthew's story of the nativity, as soon as Jesus is born, there are people who try to kill him.

Then, as now, there are people who see children as a threat, or a tool to be exploited. Children are kidnapped and killed by drug lords. Young girls enslaved by sex traffickers. Boys are kidnapped in the night and forced to become child soldiers. There are those who make their living selling dangerous and addictive drugs to teens. Unscrupulous adults seduce them online with false affections and attentions. The suffering of migrant children is easy to ignore. Somehow, it has become acceptable for children to be collateral damage in war. Once again, child labor is acceptable in sweatshops and slaughterhouses, acceptable if the child is poor, foreign, or an immigrant. In the United States, gun violence is the leading cause of death for children under the age of eighteen. Eleven million children exist below the poverty line in the richest country in the world. The slaughter of the innocents continues at a pace beyond Herod's wildest imagination.

There is a grim reality to the nativity story. Christmas angels don't spend all their time singing God's glories; they also give urgent warnings that the life of the Christ Child needs to be protected. The same angels warn us that children still need to be protected if they are going to live. Their lives need to be prioritized: Joseph and Mary had to wake in the middle of the night, uproot all their plans, and leave everything behind to make a desperate run to protect the life of their child. Love needs to be prioritized and protected if it is to survive.

If you hear the scriptural voices of angels telling you the lives of the children who are the brothers and sisters of the Christ Child need to be protected, do what Joseph and Mary did. Get up! Act! Move! Waste no time wondering if this is a political ploy, or if the angels' warning is fake news. Herod is searching for children to destroy.

Fifth Day of Christmas

December 29

FEAST OF THE HOLY FAMILY

PICTURES OF THE Holy Family often paint an unreal, idealized version of what family is, or what we want it to be. The truth is families come in all different flavors, colors, traditions. A biblical look at the original Holy Family shows them to be very different than they are often portrayed.

The Holy Family started with a pregnancy out of wedlock. The Holy Family began with talk of divorce. Taxes forced the Holy Family out of their home when Mary was about to have a child. She gave birth when the Holy Family was homeless. The Holy Family were refugees, fleeing danger to keep their child safe. The Holy Family were immigrants—twice—having to learn a new language and new customs, and search for a job in a new country. The Holy Family had a runaway child. The Holy Family suffered premature death and became a single-parent family. St. Mark's Gospel tells us that when Jesus began his ministry his family came to grab him, convinced he was "out of his mind"—Mary, not being the first or last mother to think that about her child's career choice. The Holy Family saw their son arrested, tortured, and killed right before their eyes; they were helpless to save him. The Holy Family depended on the kindness of strangers to bury their son.

The Holy Family was not holy because their lives were easy. They suffered internal stresses and external persecutions as most families do. There were misunderstandings, pain, and loss. The Holy Family was holy not because they were perfect. They were holy because they met the stresses and strains of life, the pains and sufferings of being a family, with faith, hope, and love.

Families are the places where human beings don't simply learn about God:

Families are the places where we experience God.

God is present in the best and the worst that families bring.

From our family we learn safety, trust, and belonging.

We learn that we need others for survival and affection.

We learn that other people sacrifice and work for our happiness.

Within families we learn gratitude.

Families also teach us about disappointment,

for even those who love us the most can hurt us.

Within families we also learn that we hurt those that we love.

Flaws everyone in our family possesses teach us the importance of forgiveness—forgiveness, the action that is essential to love.

Within families we learn we can be selfish, greedy, thoughtless, unfaithful.

Families are places we learn to say "I'm sorry."

Families prepare us for the day we leave to start a family of our own.

Families do not live in a bubble; they live in the real world, where life is hard.

Families struggle for economic survival, cope with illness, addictions, even death.

Some families, too many, live amid corruption and war, losing members to crime and violence.

Families are the places we learn to grieve and hope for the life with God that does not end.

Because families are made up of human beings, none of them are perfect; all of them are a little bit broken, and each of them needs the grace of God.

On the Feast of the Holy Family, we pray for that grace, for God's blessing on the families we come from, the families we create, and the families from which we are estranged. As it happens, God's blessing is ours to give.

Sixth Day of Christmas

December 30

FLIGHT INTO EGYPT

Angels again trouble Joseph's dreams.

"Get up, now! There is no time to waste.
Take the child and his mother to Egypt.
Herod is searching for the child to destroy him." (Matt 2:13, paraphrased)

Even helpful angels are troublesome.

Joseph shaking Mary, finally asleep between feedings,
informing her the angels are back.

Pack up Jesus and whatever fits on a donkey.

Keep the baby as quiet as you can.

Slipping away before sunrise, they walk to Egypt.

Google Maps says it is a distance of four-hundred-odd miles.

Sand, robbers, and wild beasts, between them and safety.

Sixth Day of Christmas

The Christ Child shares our experience as exiles.

To some extent we are all refugees, searching for a place of rest,

dependent on the kindness of strangers,

fleeing dangers within and without.

If we saw each other as companions on our life journey,

we would be less lonely.

As it is, and not without reason, we tend to look on others as Herod's soldiers, their mission: to take what is ours—even our life.

We might reflect more deeply on the ministry of parents to protect

their children from those who seek to harm them by

using them to fulfill their greed and lusts.

Protection is the emotion gripping immigrant parents,

Propelling them to walk or sail impossible distances,

crossing unwelcoming borders, all to keep their children safe

from those who seek, in one way or another, to kill them.

If I were sitting down to a morning cappuccino with Pope Francis,

I would suggest that he insert into the Christmas season

the Feast of the Flight into Egypt, or we could call it,

Jesus, Mary, Joseph—the Holy Refugees.

Seventh Day of Christmas

December 31

NEW YEAR'S EVE

You may be a New Year's Eve person, ready to party, or maybe not.

New Year's Eve, for my family, was another occasion for a festive dinner.

Roasted fresh ham with crackling skin was on the menu.

It was a favorite of my mother's sister, Renee, and her husband, Frank.

After a boring evening of watching Guy Lombardo on TV (look him up),

the family, led by Uncle Frank, had a midnight parade of silver sparklers.

Imagine what the neighbors thought.

Seventh Day of Christmas

Before your festive evening begins, do yourself this favor.
Over the Christmas holidays, certainly over the year,
someone has annoyed you, angered you, disappointed
you.
I am talking about people you actually know.
People who have hurt your feelings, or you, theirs.
It is not a good idea to carry grudge or guilt,
Disappointment or doubt, into the New Year.

Forgiveness may be too much to ask on short notice.
It may not be warranted, not without repentance.
At the very least, do your best to let the memory go:
*"Do not let the sun go down on your anger, and do not make
room for the devil"* (Eph 4:26–27).
Last year was hard enough without dragging all that into
the New Year.
Be gentle with yourself and others.
What you cannot bring yourself to forgive, in others or
yourself,
entrust to God's mercy.
Allow God to soften hearts and heal consciences.
Pray for this gift, then go out and party to your heart's
content.

Happy New Year!

Eighth Day of Christmas

January 1

NEW YEAR'S DAY

Einstein's theory of relativity states time is not what we think it is.

Time is not absolute, and its measurement and experience is relative to space and the observer.

All well and good for Einstein,

but the rest of us find time a hard, unyielding reality.

The exact time and date of our birth and death is recorded.

In between, we mark time: birthdays, anniversaries, holidays,

the passing of seasons.

The moment when we met the love of our life and when we lost them.

The time when we had a job or lost one or retired.

Eighth Day of Christmas

We know how long we have been in recovery,
how long afflicted with ailments;
we ask, when grievously ill,
how much time we have left.
We rush to be on time and are annoyed with the tardy.
We talk about the good old times,
looking back in nostalgia, or we look forward to better
times.
Time can drag on or fly by. Time heals some wounds
while others fester under the drip-drip of time.

It seems as if time is all we have.
When all is said and done, we have precious little of it.
So many, too many, cut down before the prime of life.
So many, too many, never getting a start in life.
So many, too many, unable to enjoy the rest their years
merit.

Those of us who measure time so precisely,
who guard its passing so jealously,
what do we do with a God for whom time is infinite?
"A thousand years are as a night" sings the psalm.
All well and good for God, but we have this new year.
For some of us, this will be our last year for something,
for someone, maybe for everything.

A new year is called the year of the Lord.
Whether it will be a year of our Lord, or not,
remains to be seen.

Comfort and Joy

A year of our Lord must be carved out of the morass
of violence, indifference, and greed
flooding the news and dominating political discourse.
It will be a year of our Lord only if we
actively chip away at the accretions of our worst,
revealing the original masterpiece of love
God creates and intends for humankind.
The tools with which this New Year are to be carved are
at hand:
mercy, compassion, forgiveness, a thirst for justice and
righteousness,
humility that places others' needs above my wants,
courage to suffer love's pains for the sake of another,
the stubborn trust that I am loved by God despite
contempt—
be it from others or my own self-hatred—
the yearning for hope, joy, passion, play,
the desire to learn,
the need to create beauty—
these are the tools that can be found in the life of Jesus.

They are also found in other faith traditions,
whose spiritual leaders humbly, selflessly, generously,
seek to love and serve God.
These are not the tools of the selfish and powerful.
These tools belong to the loving, our tools, our lives.
May we live them with God's blessing:

Eighth Day of Christmas

"The Lord bless you and keep you;

The Lord make his face to shine upon you, and be gracious to you;

The Lord look on you kindly, and give you peace." (Num 6:24–26)

Happy New Year!

Ninth Day of Christmas

January 2

HOME

TIME TO BLESS your home for the New Year! Once upon a time, even today, depending on your country, each home receives a blessing from the journeying Three Kings. In the twelve days between Christmas and Epiphany, priests would visit each home in the parish and inscribe with chalk a blessing on the doorway. It looks like this:

$$20 + C + M + B + 25$$

The first two integers of the upcoming year, blessings from each of the three kings—Casper, Melchior, and Balthasar—followed by the last two integers of the year. The kings who brought gold, frankincense, and myrrh bestow the blessings of prosperity, health, and holiness on those who cross the threshold. It was a practical way for the priests to visit the people of the parish and keep in touch with their lives while enjoying a strudel and coffee. A new tradition has arisen where children dress up as one of the kings and chalk the blessing over the doorway of every house, apartment, or room in which someone makes their home.

Whether this is your tradition or not, whether you use chalk or not, pray a blessing on your home for the New Year. Home is where you long to be at the end of the day, to rest, eat, laugh, love, sleep. It is where you can close the door and dance or worry, be sad or angry, or just be alone. At home you are yourself with no one to impress. Home may be shared with those you love, where you make and treasure memories. You invite friends home to share your space, to relax, to play. People bring the love of their life home, to meet the family, to see where and how they live. Perhaps, they become engaged at home, often during Christmastide.

Homes are troubled as well, for they house our sorrow and angers, our griefs and fears. So potent are these powers, home can be fractured, broken, lonely, toxic, home in name only. We are driven to run away from such a home. Unnecessary hours are spent at work or some other activity just to avoid returning home. Children who have lost their parents' love can be thrown out of their home to live as best they can on the street. They join the ranks of the homeless. Not just children suffer loss of home. Adults who have lost their love divorce from one another and their home.

Can you think of anything more worthy of blessing than your home? Now, before the New Year gets any older, pray your best blessing on your home, that it be a place of safety, a refuge and strength. Pray the Holy Spirit to dwell within, to ease and heal whatever conflicts and ills there may be. Pray that the blessing of the three kings—prosperity, health, and holiness—may be yours.

Pray God bless and keep you and all who cross your threshold with comfort and joy.

Tenth Day of Christmas

January 3

THANK-YOU NOTES

MY PARENTS INSISTED we write thank-you notes for every gift received before we returned to school. This was a waste of a perfectly good play day. If this were not bad enough, valuable, rare, priceless, cash received for Christmas was requisitioned to purchase thank-you cards and stamps. This taxation of gratitude simmered in my tiny heart, powerless to resist decrees from Caesar Augustus.

My Aunt Sophie lives in my memory as a gentle, generous woman, who made with her own hands the best ice cream sodas known to humanity. These treasures she would sneak into our hands when grandparents and parents were not looking. We could always count on her for something extra.

I have a vivid Christmas Eve recollection of opening her gift, an elaborately wrapped box. She smiled ear to ear anticipating my delight. Under the tissue paper lay a deep blue dress shirt, and wait for it, a royal blue satin tie, on which was hand-painted the head of a horse, wearing a real orange feather that stuck up out of the tie!

It is interesting, isn't it, how slowly time can move, and how many thoughts pop out of your brain in an emergency? I attended a school where boys wore shirts and ties. I imagined myself walking, as one walks to the gallows, into my classroom wearing this radiant blue shirt adorned by a horse who sported a real orange feather. Shame, everlasting, unrecoverable shame, lay before me. A dead man, I looked up and saw Aunt Sophie's face alight with glee, and over her shoulder, strategically positioned, my father's face, firing grim determination and warning. I took the only path that lay before me and gushed thanks at my Aunt Sophie, who responded with a massive, benevolent hug.

One week later, scrawling a thank-you note for Aunt Sophie's tie, I learned a gift's value is measured by the intention of the giver. From that point to this, when I am fortunate enough to receive a gift or compliment, I say thank you.

"Thank you" reorients me to the kindness of others, the priceless value of their gift. Of all the gifts I received that Christmas Eve, and many other Christmas Eve's besides, the only one I remember is Aunt Sophie's tie.

Eleventh Day of Christmas

January 4

MAGI ON THE WAY

MAGI, ASTROLOGERS, wise men, three kings, call them what you will, but they are the gift givers of Christmas for much of the world. Their gifts of gold, frankincense, and myrrh are bestowed on the Feast of the Epiphany, January 6. Anticipation of what gifts will be received sweeten many dreams, and the bestowers of gifts are heartily welcomed.

In my box of clippings is a story of another wise man from the East, bringing gifts to the Christ Child. In this case, a police officer from someplace in Massachusetts was summoned to a local grocery store where a woman was being held for not scanning all the groceries she put into her bag. The officer saw two small children, about the same age as his own children. These waifs belonged to the mother who was stealing to feed them Christmas dinner. Sternly, the officer told the woman never to come back to that store, took them to another grocery store and bought them a $250 gift card with which to purchase groceries. "I could not imagine going to a grocery store and not being able to feed my children," the officer said. Was this gift not greater than gold, frankincense, and myrrh? Have I given a gift as valuable?

Twelfth Day of Christmas

January 5

HOW TO BE A MAGI IN SIX EASY LESSONS

*L*OOK UP! You cannot be a Magi if you are always looking down. As a priest/psychologist, I am in favor of meditation and introspection. But I cannot be a Magi if I am only looking at myself. I have to look up and out of myself, out of my own experience, into the unknown, into the land of hope where stars dwell and imagination has room to sail.

Don't think you have all the answers. This caveat is especially true for those of us who are religious. Religious confidence can blind me to the fact that I have much more to learn about God. I am more like King Herod than I think, the master of my own universe, I know what belongs and what doesn't—absolutely. My religious knowledge, doctrine if you will, is supposed to be a door open to the fresh air of the Spirit, not a door slammed shut against the movement of the Living God.

Get used to the journey. Stars are not static, they do not remain in one place, the earth rotates and evolves, I cannot follow the star if I refuse to change. Even if I never move a mile from where I was born, my soul must be a world traveler, seeking out new people, new ideas, new ways of being, new experiences, new ways of being touched by God.

Don't journey alone. You may start out by yourself, but others are also looking to follow the star. I have less chance of getting lost, of surviving danger, if I journey in a caravan. The people I am journeying with may have different names for the star I am following, speak different languages, have different shades of skin, eat strange foods, employ unusual modes of travel, describe their hopes uniquely. We have something to learn from one another. We are not meant to travel alone, and together we have more gifts to offer.

Hearts should "throb and overflow." That's what the prophet Isaiah says (60:1–6). You are on the right path, have followed the right star, and have reached your destination when your heart throbs and overflows. When you have found your heartthrob, give everything you have and are, let your gold, frankincense, and myrrh overflow in thanksgiving. That is what worship is.

Go home by another route. You cannot retrace your steps. Once your heart throbs, you are never the same. Giving changes you. You become responsible for your love and must do everything possible to protect it from the King Herods of the world who come only to seek and destroy. Your journey must continue, for without knowing it, you have become a star.

Epiphany

January 6

HERE COMES EVERYBODY

IN ST. MATTHEW'S Gospel, Magi from the East
came to Jerusalem asking where they might find the
newborn child—the King of the Jews. They had observed
his star at its rising, and following it here, were asking
for directions. We know little about the Magi; we do not
know if they were men or women. Only later were they
portrayed as kings to offer a more perfect contrast with
King Herod who would seek the child not to worship but
to destroy him. What we do know is that they were out-
siders, pagans, not observant Jews. Yet they were the
ones searching for the Christ while observant people like
ourselves were not looking, and in fact felt threatened
when the Christ did arrive. Part of Matthew's artistry in
observation is that not only were nonobservant pagans
the first to seek him out, but a nonobservant pagan centu-
rion and his fellow soldiers would be the first to proclaim,
"Truly, this man was God's son" (Matt 27:54).

It is not an accident that Christmastide ends pointing us
outward, toward people of goodwill who do not share our
religion, culture, color, or way of life but who search for

God and are loved by God. The Christ comes for all and is found in all. The scripture Jesus read proclaims, "the glory of the Lord shall be revealed, and all people shall see it together" (Isa 40:5). This is the story of the Magi.

I can't remember the name of this Spanish Christmas movie; I wish I could so I could properly attribute it. The story is about a father whose young son, six or seven years of age, wants the dress of a fairy princess for Epiphany. Aghast, the father tells his son that this is no fit present for a boy and the three kings will not bring such a gift. If the boy persists in asking, he will receive nothing. The boy will not back down, nor will his father relent. The father, who truly loves his son, brings him to the toy section of a department store and shows him all the games, soldiers, soccer balls, basketballs, and LEGO sets that are fun, acceptable presents.

The boy prefers the girls toy section and the selection of dresses for the fairy princess. In desperation, the papa brings his son to the stand where the three kings receive children as does Santa Claus in the United States. He is sure the kings will tell the boy they will bring no such dress on Epiphany. Seated on the lap of one of the kings, the boy pours out his heart describing the sparkly dress that is his heart's desire. When the boy is finished, his papa goes to the king and frantically whispers, "What should I do?" The king replies, "A truly wise man would bring the dress."

On Epiphany morning, the ecstatic boy opens the gift from the kings containing his dress, crown, and wand topped with a star. Imagine the boy's surprise when his papa opens his present from the kings, containing a similar dress, crown, and star wand. Together, father and son, dressed alike, walk hand in hand down the street.

Many will find this story blasphemous, and I admit I was taken aback when I saw it. As I think on it now, I am less shocked. The Epiphany message is God's desire that everyone experience in the Christ comfort and joy.